PURPOSE *for*
EVERYDAY
LIVING

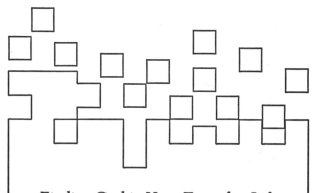

Finding God in Your Everyday Life
Mothers

CRISWELL FREEMAN

PURPOSE *for*
EVERYDAY
LIVING

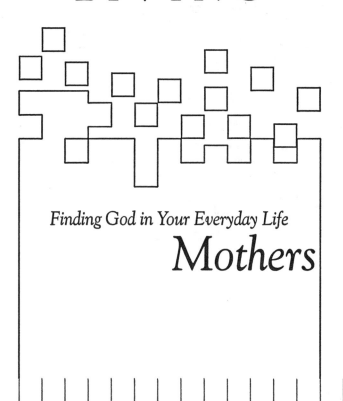

Finding God in Your Everyday Life

Mothers

The quoted ideas expressed in this book (but not scripture verses) are not, in all cases, exact quotations, as some have been edited for clarity and brevity. In all cases, the author has attempted to maintain the speaker's original intent. In some cases, quoted material for this book was obtained from secondary sources, primarily print media. While every effort was made to ensure the accuracy of these sources, the accuracy cannot be guaranteed. For additions, deletions, corrections or clarifications in future editions of this text, please contact Paul Shepherd, Editor in Chief for Elm Hill Books.
Email pshepherd@elmhillbooks.com

Products from Elm Hill Books may be purchased in bulk for educational, business, fundraising, or sales promotional use. For information, please email SpecialMarkets@ThomasNelson.com.

Scripture quotations marked (NKJV) are taken from *The Holy Bible*: New King James Version (NKJV). Copyright © 1979, 1980, 1982 by Thomas Nelson, Inc. Used by permission. All rights reserved.

Cover Design by Karen Phillips
Page Layout by Bart Dawson

Purpose for Everyday Living: Mothers ISBN 1-4041-8540-2

TABLE OF CONTENTS

God has a plan for everything, including you. As a part of that plan, He intends you experience abundance in this life, *and* throughout all eternity. But perhaps, as a concerned mother with too many commitments and too little time, *your* vision of God's plan is not as clear as you would like. If so, this book is intended to help.

The ideas on these pages are intended as tools to assist you in discovering the unfolding plans and purposes God has in store for you. This text does not attempt to answer every question concerning your particular situation; instead, it gives you Biblically-based, time-tested directions for the journey ahead.

If you sincerely seek God's guidance for your life, He will give it. But He will make His revelations known to you in a way and in a time of *His* choosing, not yours. So, if you're sincerely seeking to know God's will for your life, don't be worried if you haven't yet received a "final" answer. The final answer, of course, will come not in this world, but in the next.

If you're a mother who has encountered circumstances you don't fully understand, you are not alone. Perhaps you have endured setbacks, disappointments, or worse. If so, you have already discovered that worrying about life's problems doesn't fix them. So, instead of fretting about the future, open your heart to God in the present moment. Listen to Him, and do the work He has placed before you. Then, rest assured, if you genuinely trust God and accept the salvation of His only begotten Son, God's plans for you will be as perfect as His love.

THE SEARCH FOR PURPOSE: WHO'S GOT THE TIME?

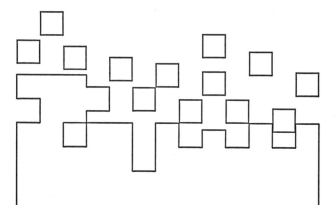

To everything there is a season,
A time to every purpose
under heaven.
Ecclesiastes 3:1 NKJV

American writer Helen Hunt Jackson observed, "The woman who creates and sustains a home is a creator second only to God." How true. But it is also worth noting that, unlike God, the woman who creates and sustains the home may have very little time for anything else!

As a loving mother, you make countless sacrifices for your family. Those sacrifices require time. If you're not careful, you'll invest so much time and energy meeting the demands of everyday life, you won't invest any time in yourself.

Time is a nonrenewable gift from God. How will you use it? You know from experience that you should invest some time each day in yourself. But finding time to do so is easier said than done. As a busy mom, you may have difficulty investing large blocks of time in much-needed thought and self-reflection—the demands of your family may simply be too great. Even if you can't block out *hours* for yourself, you can block out *minutes*—and you should.

God has big plans for you and your family. Discovering those plans will require trial and error, meditation and prayer, faith and perseverance. The moments of silence you claim for yourself will help you gather your thoughts *and* sense direction from your Creator.

Each waking moment holds the potential to think a creative thought or offer a heartfelt prayer. If you're a mother with too many demands, and too few hours in which to meet them, remain calm and don't fret. You may rest assured that when you sincerely seek to discover God's purpose for your life, He will respond in marvelous and surprising ways. Remember: this is the day He has made. He has filled it with countless opportunities to love, to serve, and to seek His guidance. Seize those opportunities today, and keep seizing them every day you live.

Most mothers are instinctive philosophers.
Harriet Beecher Stowe

An ounce of mother is worth a ton of priest.
Spanish Proverb

What the mother sings to the cradle
goes all the way down to the coffin.
Henry Ward Beecher

A mother is the holiest thing alive.
Samuel Taylor Coleridge

More than any other human relationship, overwhelmingly more, motherhood means being instantly interruptible, responsive, responsible.

—

Tillie Olsen

Let us live with urgency. Let us exploit
the opportunity of life. Let us not drift.
Let us live intentionally.
Raymond Ortlund

Life is not a journey you want to
make on autopilot.
Paula Rinehart

Time wasted is a theft from God.
Henri Frédéric Amiel

Life's unfolding stops for no one.
Kathy Troccoli

It is now and in this world that we must live.
André Gide

Time is so precious that God
deals it out only second by second.
Fulton J. Sheen

Time deals gently only with those
who take it gently.
Anatole France

*May you live all
the days of your life.*
—
Jonathan Swift

We must use time creatively and forever
realize that the time is always ripe to do right.
Nelson Mandela

Consider every day as a new beginning,
the first day of your life,
and always act with the same fervor.
St. Anthony of Padua

We all find time to do what we really want.
William Feather

God gave you this glorious day.
Don't disappoint Him. Use it for His glory.
Marie T. Freeman

Turn Down the Noise, Turn Up Your Thoughts

So much noise and so little time! In today's world, we are bombarded with instant messages, ubiquitous communications, blaring music, and unlimited information. Perhaps you've allowed this noise to fill every waking moment of your life. If so, it's time to click off the radio, the television, the computer, and the cell phone—for awhile. Try this experiment: the next time you're driving alone in your automobile, do so without radio, CD's, or cell phones. Then, have a quiet talk with God about His plans for your life. You may be surprised to discover that sometimes the most important answers are the ones you receive in silence.

FINDING GOD'S PURPOSE

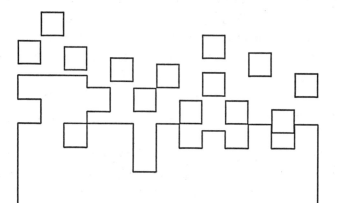

*You will show me the path of life;
in Your presence is fullness of joy;
at Your right hand are pleasures
forevermore.*
Psalm 16:11 NKJV

Life is best lived on purpose, not by accident: the sooner we discover what God intends for us to do with our lives, the better. But God's purposes aren't always clear to us. Sometimes, the responsibilities of caring for our loved ones leave us precious little time to discern God's will for ourselves. At other times, we struggle mightily against God, in a vain effort to find success and happiness through our own means, not His.

Whenever we struggle against God's plans, we suffer. When we resist God's calling, our efforts bear little fruit. Our best strategy, therefore, is to seek God's wisdom and follow Him wherever He chooses to lead. When we do so, we are blessed.

As a loving mother, you know intuitively that God has important plans for you and your family. But how can you know precisely what God's intentions are? The answer, of course, is that even the most well-intentioned believers face periods of uncertainty about the direction of their lives. So, too, will you.

When you arrive at one of life's inevitable crossroads, that is precisely the moment when you should turn your thoughts and prayers toward God. When you do, He will make Himself known to you in a time and manner of His choosing.

Are you earnestly seeking to discern God's purpose for your life? If so, these pages are intended as a reminder of several important facts: 1. God has a plan for your life; 2. If you seek that plan sincerely and prayerfully, you will find it; 3. When you discover God's purpose for your life, you will experience abundance, peace, joy, and power—God's power—the only power that really matters.

When God speaks to you through the Bible,
prayer, circumstances, the church,
or in some other way, he has a purpose
in mind for your life.
Henry Blackaby and Claude King

You can believe in Jesus Christ as your Savior,
make heaven and miss hell, but never realize
the power that God intended for
you to know in this life.
Angela Thomas

The study of inspired Scripture is
the chief way of finding our duty.
St. Basil the Great

It helps to resign as the controller of your fate. All that energy we expend to keep things running right is not what keeps things running right.

—

Anne Lamott

It's incredible to realize that what we do
each day has meaning in
the big picture of God's plan.
Bill Hybels

Blessed are those who know what on
earth they are here on earth to do
and set themselves about
the business of doing it.
Max Lucado

If we are ever going to be or do anything
for our Lord, now is the time.
Vance Havner

Only God's chosen task for you will ultimately
satisfy. Do not wait until it is too late to
realize the privilege of serving Him in
His chosen position for you.
Beth Moore

*People may make plans in their minds,
but the Lord decides what they will do.*
Proverbs 16:9 NCV

Never place a period where God
has placed a comma.
Mother Teresa

Never confuse motion with action.
Ben Franklin

If God declares what it means to be human,
then our lives are not the meaningless
collections of unrelated events they
so often appear to be.

Stanley Grenz

The one supreme business of life is to
find God's plan for your life and live it.

E. Stanley Jones

God wants to make something beautiful of
our lives; our task—as God's children
and as our children's parents—is to let Him

Jim Gallery

Never be afraid to trust an unknown future
to a known God.

Corrie ten Boom

Are you serious about wanting
God's guidance to become
the person he wants you to be?
The first step is to tell God
that you know you can't
manage your own life;
that you need his help.

—

Catherine Marshall

Open Yourself Up To God

Perhaps you have been overly anxious to impose your own plans upon the world. If so, it's time to open yourself up to God. If you have been struggling against God's will for your life, you have invited unwelcome consequences into your own life *and* into the lives of your loved ones. A far better strategy is to consult God earnestly and consistently *before* you embark upon the next stage of your life's journey.

THE DAILY JOURNEY: DAILY PRAYER AND MEDITATION

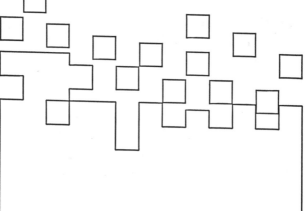

Speak, for Your servant hears.
1 Samuel 3:10 NKJV

Your search to discover God's purpose for you is not a destination; it is a continuing journey that will unfold every day of your life. And that is exactly how often you should seek direction from your Creator: every day, without exception.

Daily prayer and meditation are a matter of priority and habit. You must willingly prioritize your time by carving out quiet moments with God. You must form the habit of daily worship. When you do, you'll discover no time is more precious than the silent moments you spend with your Heavenly Father.

God promises the prayers of believers can accomplish great things. God promises He answers prayer (although *His* answers are not always in accordance with *our* desires). God invites us to be still and feel His presence. So pray. Start praying before the sun comes up. Keep praying until you fall off to sleep at night. Pray about matters great and small; and be watchful for the answers God most assuredly sends your way.

Is prayer an integral part of your daily life, or is it a hit-or-miss routine? Do you "pray without ceasing," or is your prayer life an afterthought? Do you regularly pray in the solitude of the early morning darkness, or do you bow your head only when others are watching?

The quality of your spiritual life will be in direct proportion to the quality of your prayer life. Prayer changes things, and it changes you. Today, instead of turning things over in your mind, turn them over to God in prayer. Instead of worrying about your next decision, ask God to lead the way. Don't limit your prayers to meals or to bedtime; pray constantly. God is listening. He wants to hear from you. You most certainly need to hear from Him.

Each time, before you intercede, be quiet first
and worship God in His glory. Think of what
He can do and how He delights to hear
the prayers of His redeemed people.
Think of your place and privilege in Christ,
and expect great things!

Andrew Murray

Real power in prayer flows only when
a person's spirit touches God's spirit.

Catherine Marshall

Prayer is an expression of a clear,
simple relationship with God.

Henry Blackaby

There will be no power in our lives
apart from prayer.
Angela Thomas

Prayer shouldn't be casual or sporadic,
dictated only by the needs of the moment.
Prayer should be as much a apart of
our lives as breathing.
Billy Graham

The manifold rewards of a serious,
consistent prayer life demonstrate clearly
that time with our Lord should be
our first priority.
Shirley Dobson

Never underestimate the power that
comes when a parent pleads with
God on behalf of a child.
Max Lucado

God's command to "pray without ceasing" is
founded on the necessity we have of his grace
to preserve the life of God in the soul,
which can no more subsist one moment
without it than the body can without air.
John Wesley

Prayer isn't just preparation for the battle;
prayer is the battle.
Bob Logan

When any needy heart begins to truly pray,
heaven itself stirs in response.
Jim Cymbala

As a mother, my job is to take care of the possible and trust God with the impossible.

—

Ruth Bell Graham

Wasted time of which we are later ashamed,
temptations we yield to, weaknesses, lethargy
in our work, disorder and lack of discipline
in our thoughts and in our interaction
with others—all these frequently have their
root in neglecting prayer in the morning.
Dietrich Bonhoeffer

I live in the spirit of prayer; I pray as I walk,
when I lie down, and when I rise.
And, the answers are always coming.
George Mueller

Prayer is the way to open ourselves to God,
and the way in which He shows us our unstable
hearts and begins to strengthen them.
St. Teresa of Avila

To talk to his children about God,
a person needs to first talk to God
about his children.
Edwin Louis Cole

Indeed, wisdom and discernment are
among the natural results of
a prayer-filled life.
Richard Foster

Prayer is never the least we can do;
it is always the most!
A. W. Tozer

There are some forms of spiritual life which are
not absolutely essential, but prayer is
the very essence of spirituality.
C. H. Spurgeon

Some people think God does not like to
be troubled with our constant asking.
But, the way to trouble God is not
to come at all.
D. L. Moody

Prayer thrives in the atmosphere of
true devotion.
E. M. Bounds

As is the business of tailors to make clothes
and cobblers to make shoes, so it is
the business of Christians to pray.
Martin Luther

*Happy is the child who happens
in upon his parent from time
to time to see him on his knees,
or going aside regularly,
to keep times with the Lord.*
—

Larry Christenson

Become a Family of Early Risers

Do you make time each morning for a time of devotional reading and prayer? Or do you stay up until the wee hours and sleep as late as possible? If you and your family members are staying up late and sleeping through the early morning hours, perhaps it's time to rearrange your schedule. If your children are like most kids, they will stay up until sunrise—if you let them. But you, as a thoughtful parent, can teach your children the wisdom of Ben Franklin's familiar adage: "Early to bed, early to rise, makes a man healthy, wealthy, and wise."

If your work schedule requires you to sleep during the day, at least you'll have a good reason for missing out on those quiet moments before the rest of the world awakens. But if you or your children are staying up late in order to watch "just one more show" on TV, do everybody a favor: click off the television and go to bed. As Ben Franklin also observed, "The early morning hath gold in its mouth."

FINDING PURPOSE AS A MOTHER

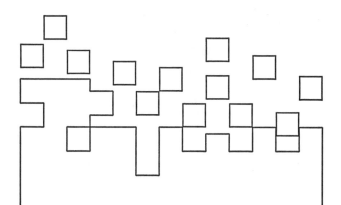

*For I know the thoughts that I think toward you,
says the LORD, thoughts of peace and not of evil,
to give you a future and a hope.*
Jeremiah 29:11 NKJV

The stay-at-home mother described herself this way: "I'm *just* a mom." That's like saying, "I'm *just* an astronaut," or "I'm *just* a Supreme Court Justice. Motherhood is not *just* another job. It's one of *the most important jobs* in God's creation.

Every child is a priceless gift from the Creator. With that gift comes immense responsibility. As a mother, you understand the critical importance of raising your children with love, with discipline, and with God. You know that your overriding purpose—whether you are a stay-at-home mom or a mom who supports her family in the workplace—is to care for your children.

As a loving mother, you appreciate the profound responsibility of being a parent. But perhaps you feel God is also calling you to honor Him in other ways, too. Perhaps your children have grown up and left the nest. If so, you may choose to begin a time of heartfelt prayer and spiritual exploration. As you consider God's purpose for your own life, you will undoubtedly consider how your plans will effect the most important people God has entrusted to your care: your loved ones (whether they happen to be three years old or 103 years young).

No family is perfect, and neither is yours. Yet, in spite of the inevitable challenges of family life, your clan is God's gift to you. That little band of men, women, kids, and babies comprises a priceless treasure on temporary loan from the Father above. As you prayerfully seek God's direction, remember He has important plans for your home life as well as your professional life. It's up to you to act—and to plan—accordingly.

*The woman is the heart
of the home.*

—

Mother Teresa

There is no greater place of ministry, position,
or power than that of a mother.
Phil Whisenhunt

For three years, I felt like all I did was pick up
toys, coordinate naps, and kiss boo-boos.
But I began to realize that there was a whole
other level to my life and that I'd never had
a more important job: I was teaching
my children how to respond to God.
Lisa Whelchel

The mother is and must be, whether she knows
it or not, the greatest, strongest,
and most lasting teacher her children have.
Hannah Whitall Smith

Train up a child in the way
he should go, and when he is old
he will not depart from it.
—

Proverbs 22:6 NKJV

The role of mother is probably
the most important career
a woman can have.
Janet Mary Riley

Being a full-time mom is the hardest job
I've ever had, but it is also the best job
I've ever had. The pay is lousy,
but the rewards are eternal.
Lisa Whelchel

Focus on Purposes, Not Wishes

As you consider God's plan and purpose for you and your family, ask yourself this question: "Is this *my* wish list or God's?" If you're struggling mightily to keep up with the Jones, you may be struggling in vain. But if you set your personal wish list aside and instead seek God's purposes for your life, He will lead you in the direction you should go. Never allow greed, fear, selfishness, or pride to separate you from the will of God. Seek His kingdom first, and then have faith He will provide all the things that you *need*, even if He does not grant all the things you *want*.

THE CHRIST-CENTERED FAMILY

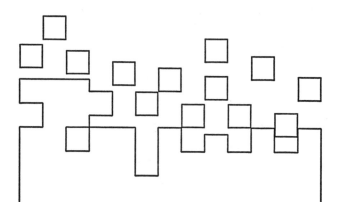

Choose for yourselves this day
whom you will serve . . . as for me
and my house, we will serve the LORD.
Joshua 24:15 NKJV

A loving family is a treasure from God. If God has blessed you with a close knit, supportive clan, offer a word of thanks to your Creator. He has given you one of His most precious earthly possessions. Your obligation, in response to God's gift, is to treat your family in ways that are consistent with His commandments.

You live in a competitive world, a place where life can be difficult and pressures can be intense. As those pressures build, you may tend to focus so intently upon your earthly concerns, you lose sight, albeit temporarily, of your spiritual and emotional needs (one reason why a regular daily devotional time is so important: it offers a dose of badly-needed perspective).

Even when the demands of everyday life are great, you must never forget that, as a mother, you are entrusted with a profound responsibility:

nurturing the spiritual growth of your family. Motherhood, of course, is a job like no other: at times joyous, at times exhausting. You give your family love, support, help, advice, and cooperation—for starters. You may also serve as the family's manager, banker, arbitrator, housekeeper, babysitter, cook, counselor, medic, and chauffeur. Whew! It's a big job. But with God's help, you're up to the task.

When you place God squarely in the center of your family's life—when you worship Him, praise Him, trust Him, and love Him—He will most certainly bless you and yours in ways you could have scarcely imagined.

*A good woman is the best thing
on earth.… The church owes
a debt to our faithful women
which we can never estimate,
to say nothing of the debt we
owe in our homes to
our godly wives and mothers.*

—

Vance Havner

I remember my mother, my father
and the rest of us praying together each
evening. It is God's greatest gift to the family.
Mother Teresa

The family that prays together, stays together.
Anonymous

All that I am or hope to be I owe
to my angel mother.
Abraham Lincoln

Do you want to help your children reach
the maximum potential that lies within them?
Then raise them according to the precepts
and values given to us in the Scriptures.
James Dobson

The Christian life has two different dimensions:
faith toward God and love toward men.
You cannot separate the two.
Warren Wiersbe

Mother is the name for God on the lips
and in the hearts of little children.
William Makepeace Thackeray

There is nothing more special, more precious
than time that a parent spends struggling
and pondering with God on behalf of a child.
Max Lucado

We must strengthen our commitment to model strong families ourselves, to live by godly priorities in a culture where self so often supersedes commitment to others. And, as we not only model but assertively reach out to help others, we must realize that even huge societal problems are solved one person at a time.

Chuck Colson

Let us look upon our children; let us love them and train them as children of the covenant and children of the promise. These are the children of God.

Andrew Murray

*The family circle is
the supreme conductor
of Christianity.*

—

Henry Drummond

Quality Time or Quality Time?

What is more important: quality time or quantity time? The answer is straightforward: your family needs both. As a loving mom, you must provide *high quantities* of *high-quality* time in caring for your clan. As you nurture your loved ones, you should do your very best to ensure God remains squarely at the center of your family's life. When you do, He will bless you—and yours—in ways you could have scarcely imagined.

FINDING PURPOSE IN THE WORKPLACE

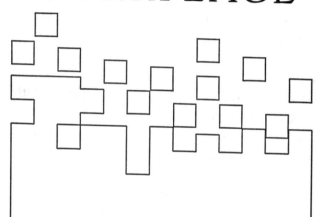

He did it with all his heart. So he prospered.
2 Chronicles 31:21 NKJV

If you're a mom who spends her entire workday at home, you need not look very far to discover the purpose behind your efforts: they're probably running through the house at this very moment!

If you're a mom who does double duty at home *and* the workplace, then you're vitally concerned with finding work you enjoy. If you've found a vocation you love, and if your efforts help make the world a better place, consider yourself doubly blessed. But if you're dissatisfied with your employment, or if you feel your professional life is not pleasing to God, there's only one thing to do: you must keep searching.

Perhaps you've been searching for work that is pleasing to other people. Perhaps you find yourself struggling in a job that is not suited to your skills. In either case, you must remember God made you exactly as you are. He did so for a very good reason: *His* reason. Therefore, you must glorify God by honoring the talents *He gave you,* not the talents *you wish He had given you.*

When you discover the work for which God created you, you'll be productive and inspired. But until you find that work, you'll have trouble generating the enthusiasm you need to be successful. Unfortunately, too many people labor in jobs for which they are ill suited or overqualified. To do so is an obvious mistake, but it's a common mistake nonetheless.

Have you found work about which you are passionate? If you work outside the home, have you discovered a vocation that inspires you to arrive at the office ten minutes early, rather than ten minutes late? Does your work help create a better world *and* a better you? If the answer to these questions is yes, consider yourself both fortunate and wise. But if the dream of meaningful work remains elusive, keep searching—and praying—until you find it.

What is the recipe for successful achievement?
Choose a career you love.
Give it the best there is in you.
Seize your opportunities.
And be a member of the team.
Ben Franklin

A job is something that you do for money.
A career is something you do because
you are inspired to do it.
Edward James Olmos

Starting out to make money is the greatest
mistake in life. Do what you feel you have
a flair for doing, and if you are
good enough at it, the money will come.
Greer Garson

*It is not a matter of thinking
a great deal but of loving
a great deal, so do whatever
arouses you most to love.*

—

St. Teresa of Avila

The time comes when you realize that you
haven't only been specializing in something—
something has been specializing in you.
Arthur Miller

Finding your particular talent or vocation is
the first step in the art of being successful.
Conrad Hilton

You usually enjoy what you're good at.
Cal Turner, Sr.

*In the long run, it makes little
difference how cleverly others
are deceived; if we are not doing
what we are best equipped to do,
there will be a core of unhappiness
in our lives which will be more
and more difficult to ignore
as the years pass.*

—

Dorothea Brande

If you want to be successful,
it's just this simple:
Know what you're doing.
Love what you're doing.
And believe in what you're doing.
—
Will Rogers

Know thy work and do it.
Thomas Carlyle

Get absolutely enthralled with something.
Throw yourself into it with abandon.
Get out of yourself. Be somebody.
Do something.
Norman Vincent Peale

The person who excels is the person who does
something for the pure love of it and doesn't
think of the commercial consequences. If you
do something, do it right, and the finances
will usually take care of themselves.
Chet Atkins

The road to happiness lies in two simple
principles: find what it is that interests you
and that you can do well, and when you find it,
put your whole soul into it every bit of energy
and ambition and natural ability you have.
John D. Rockefeller III

Don't "Settle" for Less

In terms of a career choice, most people find it is easy to "settle" for a job that is safe and familiar. Don't be like most people. After all, God didn't create you for mediocrity.

If you feel passionately about your work and that you're well suited for the task at hand, say a word of thanks. If on the other hand, you feel underemployed (or if you feel your skills might be better used in another way), ask God for the courage, the perseverance, and the wisdom you need to select a more suitable path.

AT PEACE WITH YOUR PURPOSE

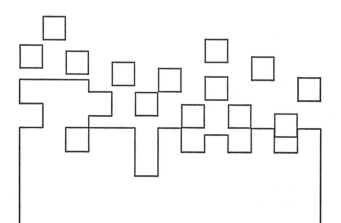

*And let the peace of God rule
in your hearts…and be thankful.*
Colossians 3:15 NKJV

For busy mothers, a moment's peace can be a scare commodity. But no matter how numerous the interruptions and demands of the day, God is ever-present, always ready and willing to offer solace to those who seek "the peace that passes all understanding."

When we accept the peace of Jesus Christ into our hearts, our lives are transformed. Because we possess the gift of peace, we can share that gift with fellow Christians, family members, friends, and associates. If on the other hand, we choose to ignore the gift of peace—for whatever reason—we simply cannot share what we do not possess.

Today, as a gift to yourself, to your family, and to your friends, claim the inner peace that is your spiritual birthright: the peace of Jesus Christ. It is offered freely; it has been paid for in full; it is yours for the asking. So ask. Then share.

Peace I leave with you,
My peace I give to you;
not as the world gives do
I give to you.
Let not your heart be troubled,
neither let it be afraid.
—
John 14:27 NKJV

Of all the rights of women,
the greatest is to be a mother.
Lin Yutang

Motherhood is the greatest privilege of life.
Mary Roper Coker

There is no more influential
or powerful role on earth than a mother's.
Charles Swindoll

*When parents find God's peace,
the blessings flow straight
down to their children.*

—

Marie T. Freeman

For Jesus peace seems to have meant not
the absence of struggle
but the presence of love.
Frederick Buechner

The better acquainted you become with God,
the less tensions you feel
and the more peace you possess.
Charles Allen

Peace with God is where all peace begins.
Jim Gallery

The joy of anything, from a blade of grass
upwards, is to fulfill its created purpose.
Oswald Chambers

Now God designed the human machine
to run on Himself. God cannot give us
happiness and peace apart from Himself,
because it is not there.
There is no such thing.
C. S. Lewis

Where the Spirit of the Lord is,
there is peace;
where the Spirit of the Lord is,
there is love.
Stephen R. Adams

That peace, which has been described
and which believers enjoy, is a participation
of the peace which their glorious Lord
and Master himself enjoys.
Jonathan Edwards

Rejoicing is a matter of obedience to God—
an obedience that will start you on
the road to peace and contentment.
Kay Arthur

The peace that Jesus gives is never engineered
by circumstances on the outside.
Oswald Chambers

*These things I have spoken to you,
that in Me you may have peace.
In the world you will have
tribulation; but be of good cheer,
I have overcome the world.*
—

John 16:33 NKJV

Peace in the Present Moment

Does peace seem to be a distant promise? It is not. God's peace is available to you this very moment *if* you place absolute trust in Him. Elisabeth Elliot writes, "If my life is surrendered to God, all is well. Let me not grab it back, as though it were in peril in His hand but would be safer in mine!" Today, let go of your concerns by turning them over to God. Trust Him in the present moment, and accept His peace—in the present moment.

TRANSITIONS:
EVERYBODY'S
GROWING UP

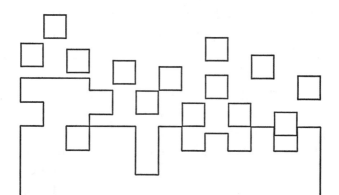

*Then He went down with them and came
to Nazareth, and was subject to them,
but His mother kept all these things in her heart.
And Jesus increased in wisdom
and stature, and in favor with God and men.*
Luke 2:51-52 NKJV

Our world is in a state of constant change and so are our families. God is not.

At times, everything around us seems to be changing: our children are growing up, we are growing older, loved ones pass on. Sometimes, the world seems to be trembling beneath our feet. But we can be comforted in the knowledge our Heavenly Father is the rock that cannot be shaken. His Word promises, "I am the LORD, I do not change" (Malachi 3:6 NKJV).

Every day we live, we mortals encounter a multitude of changes—some good, some not so good. On occasion, all of us must endure life-changing personal losses that leave us breathless. When we do, our loving Heavenly Father stands ready to protect us, to comfort us, to guide us, and, in time, to heal us.

Are you facing difficult transitions, or unwelcome adjustments? If so, please remember God is far bigger than any challenge you may face. Instead of worrying about the shifting sands of life, put your faith in the One who cannot be moved.

Are you anxious about situations you cannot control? Take your anxieties to God. Are you troubled? Take your troubles to Him. Does your world seem to be changing too fast for its own good? Remember "Jesus Christ is the same yesterday, today, and forever" (Hebrews 13:8 NKJV). Rest assured: It is precisely because your Savior does not change, that you can face the transitions of life with courage for today and hope for tomorrow.

You cannot step twice in the same river,
for other waters are continually flowing on.
Heraclitus

Weep not that the world changes—
did it keep a stable, changeless state,
it were cause indeed to weep.
William Cullen Bryant

All changes, even the most longed for,
have their melancholy; for what we leave
behind is a part of ourselves; we must die to
one life before we can enter into another!
Gail Sheehy

The secret of a happy life:
Accept change gracefully.

—

Jimmy Stewart

God loves us the way we are,
but He loves us too much
to leave us that way.
—

Leighton Ford

Only mothers can think of the future,
because they give birth to it in their children.
Maxim Gorky

Children are today's investments
and tomorrow's dividend.
Anonymous

Children are the messages we will send
to a time we will never see.
Neil Postman

*A baby is God s opinion
that the world should go on.*
—
Carl Sandburg

Every mother is like Moses.
She does not enter
the promised land.
She prepares a world
she will not see.

—

Pope Paul VI

Each child is an adventure into a better life—
an opportunity to change the old pattern
and make it new.
Hubert H. Humphrey

Every child born into the world is
a new thought of God,
an ever-fresh and radiant possibility.
Kate Douglas Wiggin

Children are the hands by which
we take hold of heaven.
—

Henry Ward Beecher

Treasure Today . . . And Use It

Time is a nonrenewable gift from God. But sometimes we treat our time here on earth as if it were not a gift at all. We may be tempted to invest our lives in trivial pursuits and petty diversions. But our Father beckons each of us to a higher calling.

An important element of our stewardship to God is the way we choose to spend the time He has entrusted to us. Each waking moment holds the potential to hug a child, do a good deed, say a kind word, or to offer a heartfelt prayer. Our challenge, as believers, is to use our time wisely in the service of God's work, and in accordance with His plan for our lives.

Today, like every day, is a special treasure to be savored and celebrated. May we—as Christians who have so much to celebrate—never fail to praise our Creator by rejoicing in this glorious day, and by using it wisely.

WHEN MOMS MUST MOVE MOUNTAINS

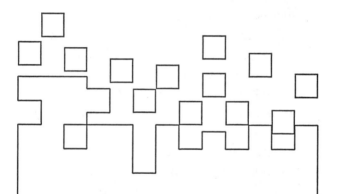

*. . . If you have faith as a mustard seed,
you will say to this mountain,
"Move from here to there," and it will move;
and nothing will be impossible for you.*
Matthew 17:20 NKJV

Sometimes, moms are expected to move mountains, especially by young children who believe, quite legitimately, mom can fix *anything*. But mothers beware: maternal mountain moving requires faith.

Every life—including yours—is a series of successes and failures, celebrations and disappointments, joys and sorrows. Every step of the way, through every triumph and tragedy, God will stand by your side and strengthen you —if you have faith in Him. Jesus taught his disciples that if they had faith, they could move mountains. You can too.

When a suffering woman sought healing by merely touching the hem of His cloak, Jesus replied, "Be of good cheer, daughter; your faith has made you well" (Matthew 9:22 NKJV). The message to believers of every generation is clear: we must live by faith today and every day. Sometimes, however, faith is in short supply, especially when we encounter circumstances that leave us discouraged or afraid.

As Christians, we have every reason to live courageously. After all, the ultimate battle has already been fought and won on the cross at Calvary. But even dedicated followers of Christ may find their courage tested by the inevitable disappointments and fears that visit the lives of believers and non-believers alike.

The next time you find your courage tested to the limit, remember to take your fears to God. If you call upon Him, you will be comforted. Whatever your challenge, whatever your trouble, God can handle it—and will.

When you place your faith, your trust— indeed your life—in the hands of your heavenly Father, you'll be amazed at the marvelous things He can do with you and through you. So strengthen your faith through praise, worship, Bible study, and prayer. Trust God's plans. With Him, all things are possible. He stands ready to open a world of possibilities to you—*if* you have faith. And now, with no further ado, let the mountain moving begin.

The Christian life is one of faith,
where we find ourselves routinely overdriving
our headlights but knowing it's okay because
God is in control and has a purpose behind it.
Bill Hybels

Faith expects from God what is
beyond all expectation.
Andrew Murray

No one is surprised over what God
does when he has faith in Him.
Oswald Chambers

*I remember my mother's
prayers . . . and they
have clung to me all my life.*
—

Abraham Lincoln

*Little faith will bring
your soul to heaven;
great faith will bring heaven
to your soul.*

—

C. H. *Spurgeon*

Walk by faith! Stop the plague of worry.
Relax! Learn to say,
"Lord, this is Your battle."
Charles Swindoll

Because God is my sovereign Lord,
I was not worried. He manages perfectly,
day and night, year in and year out,
the movements of the stars, the wheeling of
the planets, the staggering coordination of
events that goes on at the molecular level in
order to hold things together. There is
no doubt that he can manage the timing
of my days and weeks.
Elisabeth Elliot

Once we recognize our need for Jesus,
then the building of our faith begins.
It is a daily, moment-by-moment life of
absolute dependence upon Him
for everything.
Catherine Marshall

Without faith, nothing is possible.
With it, nothing is impossible.
Mary McLeod Bethune

*Faith is a beam radiating
from the face of God.*

—

St. John Eudes

*How changed our lives would be
if we could only fly through
the days on wings of
surrender and trust!*

—

Hannah Whitall Smith

Faith is two empty hands held open
to receive all of the Lord Jesus.
Alan Redpath

It is not my ability, but my response
to God's ability, that counts.
Corrie ten Boom

As God's children, we are the recipients of
lavish love—a love that motivates us
to keep trusting even when we have
no idea what God is doing.
Beth Moore

Faith is not belief without proof,
but trust without reservation.
Elton Trueblood

Fear lurks in the shadows of every area of life.
The future may look very threatening.
Jesus says, "Stop being afraid. Trust me!"
Charles Swindoll

When we are in a situation where Jesus is all
we have, we soon discover he is
all we really need.
Gigi Graham Tchividjian

Faith in faith is pointless.
Faith in a living, active God
moves mountains.
—

Beth Moore

Sometimes, the Answer Is "No"

God does not answer all of our prayers in the affirmative, nor should He. His job is not to grant all our earthly requests; His job is to offer us eternal salvation (for which we must be forever grateful).

When we are disappointed by the realities of life here on earth, we should remember our prayers are always answered by a sovereign, all-knowing God. We must trust Him, whether He answers "Yes", "No", or "Not yet".

THE POWER OF OPTIMISM

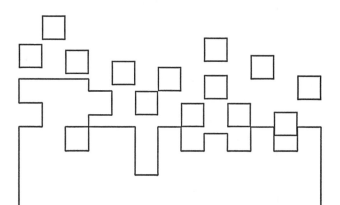

*For God has not given us a spirit of fear,
but of power and of love and of a sound mind.*
2 Timothy 1:7 NKJV

As Christian parents, we have every reason to be optimistic about life. As John Calvin observed, "There is not one blade of grass, there is no color in this world that is not intended to make us rejoice." But sometimes, rejoicing is the last thing on our minds. Sometimes, we fall prey to worry, frustration, anxiety, or sheer exhaustion, and our hearts become heavy. What's needed is plenty of rest, a large dose of perspective, and God's healing touch. But not necessarily in that order.

Because you are a conscientious mom living in a difficult world, you may find yourself pulled down by the inevitable demands and worries of everyday life in the 21st Century. Ours is a world brimming with temptations, distractions, and dangers. Sometimes, we can't help ourselves: we worry for our families, and we worry for ourselves.

If you become discouraged, exhausted, or both, then it's time to take your concerns to God. Whether you find yourself at the pinnacle of the mountain or the darkest depths of the valley, God is there. Open your heart to Him. He will lift your spirits and renew your strength.

Today, as a gift to your family and yourself, why not claim the joy that is rightfully yours in Christ? Why not take time to celebrate God's glorious creation? Why not trust your hopes instead of your fears? When you do, you will think optimistically about yourself and your world. Then you can share your optimism with others. They'll be better for it—so will you! But not necessarily in that order.

Just as clouds hide the sun,
so bad thoughts cast shadows over the soul.
St. John Climacus

Perpetual optimism is a force multiplier.
Colin Powell

When you affirm big, believe big,
and pray big, big things happen.
Norman Vincent Peale

*A mother's love
sees no impossibilities.*

—

Old Saying

The things we think are the things that feed our souls. If we think on pure and lovely things, we shall grow pure and lovely like them; and the converse is equally true.

—

Hannah Whitall Smith

The greater part of our happiness or misery
depends on our dispositions,
and not on our circumstances.
Martha Washington

Some people complain that God put thorns
on roses, while others praise Him
for putting roses on thorns.
Anonymous

A pessimist is one who makes difficulties of
his opportunities; an optimist is one
who makes opportunities of his difficulties.
Harry S Truman

An optimistic mind is a healthy mind.
Loretta Young

The world of achievement has always
belonged to the optimist.
J. Harold Wilkens

No pessimist ever discovered the secrets of
the stars or sailed to an uncharted land,
or opened a new heaven to the human spirit.
Helen Keller

It was my mother's belief—and mine—
to resist any negative thinking.
Audrey Meadows

There is wisdom in the habit of
looking at the bright side of life.
Father Flanagan

Who can ever measure the benefit
of a mother's inspiration?
Charles Swindoll

Be a Realistic Optimist

Your attitude toward the future will help create your future. So think realistically about yourself, your family, and your situation while making a conscious effort to focus on hopes, not fears. When you do, you'll put the self-fulfilling prophecy to work *for you and yours*.

THE POWER
OF
PERSEVERANCE

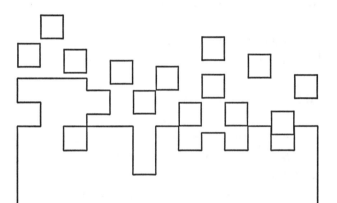

And let us not grow weary while doing good,
for in due season we shall reap
if we do not lose heart.
Galatians 6:9 NKJV

Someone once said, "Life is a marathon, not a sprint." The same can be said for motherhood. Motherhood requires courage, perseverance, determination, and an unending supply of motherly love.

As you continue to search for purpose in everyday life (while, at the same time, balancing all your maternal responsibilities), you'll encounter your fair share of roadblocks and stumbling blocks. These situations require courage, patience, and above all, perseverance. As an example of perfect perseverance, we Christians need look no further than our Savior, Jesus Christ.

Jesus, finished what He began. Despite the torture He endured, despite the shame of the cross, Jesus was steadfast in His faithfulness to God. We, too, must remain faithful, especially during times of hardship.

Are you tired? Ask God for strength. Are you discouraged? Believe in His promises. Are you frustrated or fearful? Pray as if everything depended upon God, and work as if everything depended upon you. With God's help, you will find the strength to be the kind of mother that makes her heavenly Father beam with pride.

Perhaps you are in a hurry for God to reveal His plans for your life. If so, be forewarned: God operates on His own timetable, not yours. Sometimes, God may answer your prayers with silence. When He does, you must patiently persevere. In times of trouble, you must remain steadfast, and trust in the merciful goodness of your Heavenly Father. Whatever your problem, He can handle it. Your job is to keep persevering until He does.

Keep adding, keep walking, keep advancing;
do not stop, do not turn back,
do not turn from the straight road.
St. Augustine

Only the person who follows the command of
Jesus single-mindedly, and unresistingly
lets his yoke rest upon him, finds his burden
easy, and under its gentle pressure receives
the power to persevere in the right way.
Dietrich Bonhoeffer

When problems threaten to engulf us,
we must do what believers have always done,
turn to the Lord for encouragement and solace.
As Psalm 46:1 states, "God is our refuge
and strength, an ever-present help in trouble."
Shirley Dobson

Your children learn more of
your faith during the bad times
than they do during
the good times.

—

Beverly LaHaye

Don't quit. For if you do,
you may miss the answer to your prayers.
Max Lucado

You cannot overcome if there is
nothing to overcome.
Oswald Chambers

When we do our best,
we never know what miracles await.
Helen Keller

Nothing great was ever done
without much enduring.
Catherine of Siena

There is no chance, no destiny, no fate,
that can hinder or control the firm resolve
of a determined soul.
Ella Wheeler Wilcox

We look at our burdens and heavy loads,
and we shrink from them. But, if we lift them
and bind them about our hearts,
they become wings, and on them we can rise
and soar toward God.
Mrs. Charles E. Cowman

Your life is not a boring stretch of highway.
It's a straight line to heaven. And just look at
the fields ripening along the way. Look at
the tenacity and endurance. Look at the grains
of righteousness. You'll have quite a crop
at harvest…so don't give up!
Joni Eareckson Tada

Every misfortune, every failure, every loss
may be transformed. God has the power to
transform all misfortunes into "God-sends."
Mrs. Charles E. Cowman

*Life is too short to nurse
one's misery. Hurry across
the lowlands so that you may
spend more time
on the mountaintops.*

—

Phillips Brooks

Be patient. God is using today's difficulties
to strengthen you for tomorrow.
He is equipping you. The God who makes
things grow will help you bear fruit.
Max Lucado

When I am dealing with an all-powerful,
all-knowing God, I, as a mere mortal,
must offer my petitions not only with
persistence, but also with patience.
Someday I'll know why.
Ruth Bell Graham

*In the Bible, patience is
not a passive acceptance of
circumstances. It is a courageous
perseverance in the face of
suffering and difficulty.*

—

Warren Wiersbe

God's Timing?
It's Worth the Wait

Are you anxious for God to work out His plan for your life? Who isn't? As believers, we all want God to do great things for us and through us—we want Him to do those things now. But sometimes, God has other plans. Sometimes God's timetable does not coincide with our own. It's worth noting, however, that God's timetable is always perfect.

The next time you find your patience tested to the limit, remember the world unfolds according to God's plan, not ours. Sometimes we must wait patiently, and that's as it should be. After all, think how patient God has been with us.

MOM ON
A MISSION
(FOR GOD)

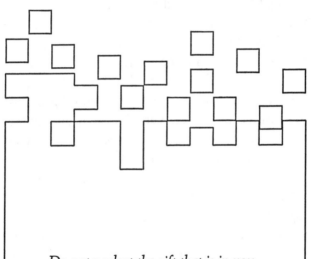

Do not neglect the gift that is in you.
1 Timothy 4:14 NKJV

Whether you realize it or not, you are on a personal mission for God. As a Christian mother, that mission is straightforward: Honor God, accept Christ as your Savior, raise your children in a loving, Christ-centered home, and be a servant to those who cross your path.

Of course, you will encounter impediments as you attempt to discover the exact nature of God's purpose for your life. But you must never lose sight of the *overriding purposes* God has established for *all* believers. You will encounter these overriding purposes again and again as you worship your Creator and study His Word.

Every day offers countless opportunities to serve God and worship Him. When you do so, He will bless you in miraculous ways. May you continue to seek God's will, may you trust His word, and may you place Him where He belongs: at the very center of your life.

Do noble things,
do not dream them all day long.
Charles Kingsley

Our Lord is searching for people who will
make a difference. Christians dare not
dissolve into the background or blend
into the neutral scenery of the world.
Charles Swindoll

The church needs people who are doers
of the Word and not just hearers.
Warren Wiersbe

Give to us clear vision that we may know where
to stand and what to stand for. Let us
not be content to wait and see what will
happen, but give us the determination
to make the right things happen.

Peter Marshall

Rest not. Life is sweeping by; go and dare
before you die. Something mighty and sublime,
leave behind to conquer time.

Goethe

Life is not a journey you want
to make on autopilot.

Paula Rinehart

What we are is God's gift to us.
What we become is
our gift to God.

—

Anonymous

You can have anything you want—
if you want it badly enough. You can be
anything you want to be, do anything you
set out to accomplish if you hold to that
desire with singleness of purpose.

Abraham Lincoln

The first thing each morning, and the last thing
each night, suggest to yourself specific ideas
that you wish to embody in your character
and personality. Address such suggestions to
yourself, silently or aloud, until they are
deeply impressed upon your mind.

Grenville Kleiser

Let us live with urgency.
Let us exploit the opportunity
of life. Let us not drift.
Let us live intentionally.
We must not trifle our lives away.
—

Raymond Ortlund

Happiness is essentially a state of going
somewhere, wholeheartedly, one-directionally,
without regret or reservation.
William H. Sheldon

No steam or river ever drives anything
until it is confined. No Niagara is ever turned
into light and power until it is harnessed.
No life ever grows until it is focused,
dedicated, disciplined.
Harry Emerson Fosdick

You cannot walk through life
without a dream or
a destination and expect
to arrive just where
you wanted to go.
—
Lisa Bevere

Be Completely Honest With Yourself

As you journey through life, you should continue to become better aquatinted with yourself. How? One way is to examine the patterns in your own life, and understand that unless you make the conscious effort to change those patterns, you're likely to repeat them. So, if you don't like some of the results you've earned, change your behaviors. The sooner you change, the sooner your results will change, too.

WORSHIPING WITH A PURPOSE

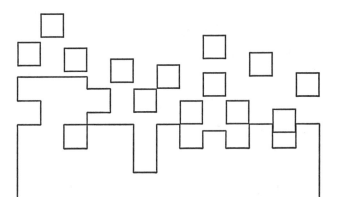

*But seek first the kingdom of God
and His righteousness, and all these things
shall be added to you.*
Matthew 6:33 NKJV

All of mankind is engaged in worship of one kind or another. The question is not whether we worship, but *what* we worship. Some of us choose to worship God. The result is a plentiful harvest of joy, peace, and abundance. Others distance themselves from God by foolishly worshiping things of this earth: fame, fortune, or personal gratification. To do so is a terrible mistake, with eternal consequences.

Whenever we place our love for material possessions above our love for God—or when we yield to the countless temptations of this world—we find ourselves engaged in a struggle between good and evil (a clash between God and Satan). Our responses to these struggles have implications that echo throughout our families and our communities.

How can we ensure we cast our lot with God? We do so, in part, by the practice of regular, purposeful worship in the company of fellow believers. When we worship God faithfully and fervently, we are blessed. When we fail to worship God, for whatever reason, we forfeit the spiritual gifts He intends for us.

We must worship our heavenly Father, not just with words, but also with deeds. We must honor Him, praise Him, and obey Him. As we seek to find purpose and meaning for our lives, we must first seek *His* purpose and *His* will. For believers, God comes first. Always first.

Praise Him! Praise Him!
Tell of His excellent greatness.
Praise Him! Praise Him!
Ever in joyful song!
Fanny Crosby

Worship is an act which develops feelings
for God, not a feeling for God which is
expressed in an act of worship. When we obey
the command to praise God in worship,
our deep, essential need to be in
relationship with God is nurtured.
Eugene Peterson

I am of the opinion that we should not
be concerned about working for God
until we have learned the meaning
and delight of worshipping Him.
A. W. Tozer

Religious activity apart from fellowship
with God is empty ritual.
Henry Blackaby

Worship is a voluntary act of gratitude
offered by the saved to the Savior,
by the healed to the Healer,
and by the delivered to the Deliverer.
Max Lucado

*Worship is about rekindling
an ashen heart into
a blazing fire.*

—

Liz Curtis Higgs

Worship is a lifestyle.
Joey Johnson

Because his spiritual existence transcends form,
matter, and location, we have the freedom to
worship him and experience his indwelling
presence wherever we are.
R. C. Sproul

There is no division into sacred and secular;
it is all one great, glorious life.
Oswald Chambers

In commanding us to glorify Him,
God is inviting us to enjoy Him.
C. S. Lewis

Worship and worry cannot live in
the same heart; they are mutually exclusive.
Ruth Bell Graham

Spiritual worship comes from our very core
and is fueled by an awesome reverence
and desire for God.
Beth Moore

Praise and thank God for who He is
and for what He has done for you.
Billy Graham

Don't ever come to church without coming
as though it were the first time,
as though it could be the best time,
and as though it might be the last time.
Vance Havner

*It is impossible to worship God
and remain unchanged.*

—

Henry Blackaby

Only on Sunday Morning?

Worship is not meant to be boxed up in a church building on Sunday morning. To the contrary, praise and worship should be woven into the very fabric of our lives.

Do you take time each day to worship your Father in heaven? Or do you wait until Sunday morning to praise Him for His blessings? The answer to this question will, in large part, determine the quality and direction of your life. So worship accordingly.

THE SEARCH CONTINUES

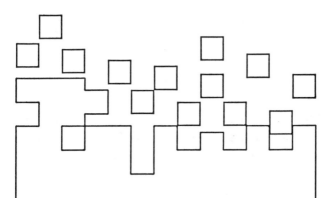

*But grow in the grace and knowledge of
our Lord and Savior Jesus Christ.
To Him be the glory both now and forever.*
2 Peter 3:18 NKJV

The journey toward spiritual maturity lasts a lifetime: As Christians, we should continue to grow in the love and knowledge of our Savior as long as we live. Norman Vincent Peale had simple advice for believers of all ages: "Ask the God who made you to keep remaking you." That advice, of course, is perfectly sound, but too often ignored.

When we cease to grow, either emotionally or spiritually, we do ourselves and our families a profound disservice. But if we study God's word, obey His commandments, and live in the center of His will, we will not be "stagnant" believers. We will be growing Christians—and that's exactly what God wants for our lives.

In those quiet moments when we open our hearts to God, the Creator who made us, keeps remaking us. He gives us direction, perspective, wisdom, and courage. The appropriate moment to accept His spiritual gifts is always this one.

*Being a mother, as far as I can
tell, is a constantly evolving
process of adapting to
the needs of your child while
also changing and growing as
a person in your own right.*
—
Deborah Insel

Keep your face upturned to Christ as
the flowers do to the sun. Look,
and your soul shall live and grow.
Hannah Whitall Smith

A person who gazes and keeps on gazing
at Jesus becomes like him in appearance.
E. Stanley Jones

With God, it isn't who you were that matters;
it's who you are becoming.
Liz Curtis Higgs

Growth is the only evidence of life.
John Henry Cardinal Newman

A Christian is never in a state of completion
but always in the process of becoming.
Martin Luther

The more completely we belong to Christ,
the more of our real selves we become.
Paula Rinehart

The mind grows by taking in,
but the heart grows by giving out.
Warren Wiersbe

You are either becoming more like Christ
every day or you're becoming less like Him.
There is no neutral position in the Lord.
Stormie Omartian

When God thought of Mother, He must have
laughed with satisfaction—so rich, so deep,
so full of power and beauty was the conception.
Henry Ward Beecher

We conclude with a dozen time-tested principles for finding your purpose in everyday life. May God richly bless you as you continue on your path.

❀ **Remember The Search for Purpose Is a Journey, Not a Destination:** Amid your changing circumstances, God will continue to reveal Himself to you, *if* you sincerely seek His will. As you journey through the stages of life, remember every new day presents fresh opportunities to seek God's will; make the conscious effort to seize those opportunities.

❀ **Pray Early and Often:** Start each day with a time of prayer and devotional readings. In those quiet moments, God will lead you. Your task, of course, is to be still, to seek His will, and to follow His direction.

❀ **Quiet Please:** Sometimes God speaks to you in a quiet voice. Usually, the small quiet voice inside, can help you find the right path for your life. Listen to that voice.

❀ **Use All the Tools That God Provides:**
As you continue to make important decisions
about your future, read God's Word every day.
Consult with trusted advisors whom God has
seen fit to place along your path.

❀ **Take Sensible Risks in Pursuit of
Personal or Professional Growth:** It is better
to attempt great things and fail, than to attempt
nothing and succeed. But make sure to avoid
foolish risks. When in doubt, reread Proverbs.

❀ **Expect Setbacks:** Your path will have
many twists and turns. When you face a setback,
don't become discouraged. When you encounter
a roadblock, be prepared to make a U-turn.
Then, start searching for a better route to your
chosen destination.

❀ **Use Your Experiences As Valued
Instructors:** Philosopher George Santayana
correctly observed, "Those who cannot
remember the past are condemned to repeat it."
Act accordingly.

❀ **Don't Settle for Second, Third, or
Fourth Best:** God has big plans for you. Don't
let Him down.

❀ **Write It Down**: If you're facing a big decision, or if you're searching for greater fulfillment from your everyday life, begin keeping a daily journal. During quiet moments, make a written record of your thoughts, your goals, your hopes, and your concerns. The simple act of writing down your thoughts will help clarify your ideas and plans.

❀ **Serve Where You Stand**: Even if you're not where you want to be, you can serve God exactly where you are. Don't underestimate the importance of your present work. Don't wait for a better day to serve God.

❀ **Find Pursuits About Which You Are Passionate**: Find work you love and causes you believe in. You'll do your best when you become so wrapped up in something, that you forget to call it work.

❀ **Have Faith and Get Busy**: Remember the words of Cyrus Curtis: "Believe in the Lord and He will do half the work—the last half."

About Criswell Freeman

Criswell Freeman's books have sold millions of copies, yet his name is largely *unknown* to the general public. *The Wall Street Journal* observed, "Normally, a tally like that would put a writer on the bestseller lists. But Freeman is hardly a household name." And that's exactly how the author likes it.

The Washington Post called Freeman "possibly the most prolific 'quote book' writer in America." With little fanfare, Dr. Freeman has compiled and edited well over a hundred titles that have now sold over 8,000,000 copies.

Freeman began his writing career as a self-help author (his first book was entitled *When Life Throws You a Curveball, Hit It*). Today, Freeman's writings focus on the Good News of God's Holy Word. Criswell is a Doctor of Clinical Psychology (he earned his degree from the Adler School of Professional Psychology in Chicago). He earned his undergraduate degree at Vanderbilt University. Freeman also attended classes at The Southern Baptist Theological Seminary in Louisville where he studied under the noted pastoral counselor Wayne Oates.

Criswell lives in Nashville, Tennessee. He is married and has two daughters.